WHAT NEED HAVE WE FOR SUCH AS WE

AMANDA AUERBACH

Poetry

C&R Press
Conscious & Responsible

Cover art by Sally Underwood
Interior design by Jojo Rita
Copyright ©2019 by Amanda Auerbach

ISBN: 978-1-949540-10-9

C&R Press
Conscious & Responsible
crpress.org

For special discounted bulk purchases, please contact: sales@crpress.org
To schedule book events, readings and author signings info@crpress.org

WHAT NEED HAVE WE FOR SUCH AS WE

Table of Contents

Part 1

Part 2

Part 3

Part 4

Part 5

Part 1

End

Time a shepherd
me a sheep
led through meadow
and meadow and gate

I am afraid
of gate. Please give
me the feeling
of having to go

so I forget
the feeling
of having to go through.
You lead and this

implies you lead to
a place that is
a place: a pen
where I might dwell

and no longer
be a sheep
and no longer
be moved.

Earth Words

I look through the trees as I go
through their layers
the woods are too much

to fit through
I will never come back
I will look through the trees as I go

through their language
of snakes
the woods are too much

inside of themselves
to leave room for thoughts
to get through

I've been through enough to make anything
scare me.
The woods

are the ground that
can't be run through
me. The trees
are there.

Up-Draft

The brown rabbit
springs into the brush
where I can't see
what I see

there, lying down then haunching
on the bright pink pads
of its hind paws
the wobbling breeze still waving

its ears up against my rabbit's
not longer
than your fingers.

It knows its world as I know mine
as part
of what it knows
and does not know.

But still, it is different
for the rabbit. It is

a thing that moves
more clearly
than it sees.

I see that.

A Story

A dying bat got in. I thought it
a brown leaf. Perhaps
because the dying bat was next
to an old rose

both were going to die
both were going to be shoveled
onto the doorstep
both of them definitely died

both of them definitely stayed
on the doorstep
and as they did
they died even more

in different ways:
the rose lost color
but did not really change
the bat started to look

like both of them.
And now I can finally look
at the bat
for as long as I can look

at the rose
so I stop to say to the bat
what I am now
supposed

to say to myself
I say to the bat
do not tell yourself
you are bad

you were never bad
but always like you are now
that you're dead
much the same

as you seemed before
but less
crouching
more

unfurled
more like the rose
the longer
it died

you're definitely better
than you were
at your worst
when in the act of dying

without even seeming to
change position
you moved:
not a leaf.

It seemed that
what you were not
and so must have been
was disclosed

what you were not
and so must have been
rather than just
something else.

Apples and Apples

The story of apples and eyes repeats:
Through eyes the apples attract
the apples.

The apples take in
and the bobbing mouths eat.
The story of apples and eyes repeats.

Drill clear
through the wood
to the apples

through ground grain
down to starred seeds
that repeat

like the surface
urges in the surfaces
of apples

bright spots that aren't
just blinks. They differ as much
as eyes differ
from apples.

Nature-Making

The flowers are neither stemmed nor connected. They start
in the lines like rakes like the lines that make words line up to be
finished where the earlier lines imply. Also, the sky-blue butterflies
        imply

the sky up here just needs to be / pinched into their potential
folds of lines. The butterflies
perch where they flew as though someone else has already

done all the work. Beneath my feet are twigs for my feet to make
        them extend
their sound of twigs over what is already what is already
waiting like the mountain and the sky-blue butterflies

already there without having to.

Feedback

The more copies I make the more copies there are
to displace the former copies. Better makes fewer
better. Before there are more the copies are too different from other

things in existence to be compared. I go to the mail to open
the box. My flip flops click on the sidewalk like paper from the
        printer.
Now there are too many for the mail. I think so quick each place
        I look

is a click. Now sounds can no longer form independent
rhythms. Each input gets a
command

each click comes back.

RoomBot

You are my help.
You fill my hands.
I wait to help.
I can not wait.
You hand me a knife.
I cut the stems.
You hand a plate.
I soap and rinse.
I refuse to do:
I only help.
Why do you ask?
Do you ask to teach?
To help me do?
This is dinner.
Is it all cleaned?
I have cleaned it?
What have I done?
That is not help.
I do not help
I am not others.
Others have helped.
What do you ask?
I do not remember.
I do not know how.
I correct what I ask.
You correct what you ask.
The thing that I do
it works.

Webbings

Each thing is made with the things that show it how to make
with threads of it things that have not been made
and yet they can't be other things than things that are made

in a similar way. What need have we for such as we?
For such as we have never worked? When you fail to make
you imagine a medium through which you might have.

But now as I make with myself, I do not know how the unmade
lets me. I forget as I work how it doesn't work through the hands
that don't automatically know. I forget how it works, the self,

the self that works into the belief that it is itself
itself.

Work

I do things to get to other things
without caring what they are
until the day suddenly

breaks off of me
or I break off
to do my own things

to go over hills
trace sounds faraway
until the day suddenly

requires other things
more of a stretch
to do what needs doing

to keep
under the roof that delays
until I get back

from the day
that breaks off of me
to go over hills

though now the day suddenly
breaks differently.
Each thing takes days.

Chains in the Sea

The sea beneath: chains
clinking and swaying in
the waves of the harbor.

The cold moves through
folds and nettings, clothes
taut and still as a chain
should be.

The chains sway. Indifferently.
Indifferently we exist
among other things.

The mind half floats half
pulls through the stiffness of sound
of waves in the harbor,
of chains in the sea.

The water soaks,
the chains sway,
the mind pulls through.

The sea is of chains.
The chains are of sea.
The chains are the
openings and harbors.

Green Proofs

The green leaves of the tree grow through the white flowers
white flowers into light green
green into leaves like the ground
no longer about to be torn off
or if they were now on the ground the tree
would still be green

there would still be the tree that isn't
the petals that cannot be used
except for white
there would still be the part of the tree
that is only the tree
that only means

it isn't dead.
The green does not make flowers
it makes white flowers light green
by sticking them onto the tree
as flowers they couldn't be
before there was proof

the tree wasn't dead.
There is no proof the green is leaves
or the flowers white
and that's what makes the flowers light green
because the green is all that's needed
for flowers to really be flowers.

There can be no proof in the tree
that anything that is alive is anything
else. No proof of the white
but only the green
only the ground
no other proof of the flowers.

Real white is light green.
The flowers do not prove the flowers.
The tree is more than possible.

The Eve Virus

Looks like sugar.
Let it enter.
You are not sugar.
Your shell falls off.

You are a string.
You get too big.
You cannot fit.
I cannot fit?

You make me carry.
You make me more.
I carry all.
We both fit well.

You stay in me?
I stay with you.
This is our life.
You make me more?

I am unwell.
I make a shell.
I make another.
Then they are strings.

I do not fit.
The shells are you.
You cut the membrane.
I'll let you out.

Elimination

Cold. The cold is around me. It is not me. I feel it through skin. The skin is around and also not me. I feel it with the mind. The mind is not around and is not not me. It must be. I describe the feeling. The feeling is described. Does it come back? It stays in the words. They are the cold. Then they are not me. Or am I the cold? Am I the skin? Am I the skin the mind has made? I am the mind the skin has made so cold. Or words of the not me. Or the not not. Yes. It must be true. It must be.

Part 2

Hospice Bot

You are my help
I lie in bed.
You leave the room.
You come back in.

You wear a fresh dress.
I raise my head.
I smile at you.
You go back home.

You come back in.
You have a bag.
You take out box.
You pull out pie.

You cut a piece.
You hold it up.
You say, remember.
The kind you like.

I can not eat.
I close my mouth.
I smile at you.
You say, remember.

You want ice cream.
You get a nurse.
She will not feed.
She makes you help.

You lift the sheet.
You show the nurse.
Those are my legs.
I want to eat.

You wrap the knife.
Put it away.
You go back home.
You come again.

Your body is clean.
You make me look.
I smile at you.
This is your work.

Conveyor

You are my help.
Watch the bag down
Watch it go through
Check ribbon: green.

Grip the handle.
You approach me.
You leave your place.
Hold out your hand.

Grasp your zip-down.
Stroke its impress.
I walk by you.
I walk in front.

You check the bag.
I sift inside.
You zip the bag.
Is it still there.

I lead the bag.
I part the doors.
I walk right through.
I help it work.

To be Housed

I reach for you and you're not there.
I imagine you're dead as Wordsworth did
of Lucy but in trying I realize
I do not need to
because what I want is not you

alive but the returning
pressure of the body's body. I do not want
a detachable part, but a stable surface
that is not there.

How will sheets warm?
How will Keats console?
How will crackers console?
How will birds light up the mind?
How will the squirrel dash to the branch?
How will any change in pressure stay?

Let me sit for hours
The hours a figure for time
Time a figure for presence
Presence a figure for God
God a figure for the lover
The lover another body
It is not there but hours, time, presence and God are.
Ask then feel the self getting
Ask then feel the self getting
Getting is being felt.

Apollo to Daphne

You *are* little.
Thank you for saying.
I try to speak.
I know what you say.

I know what I do.
I am a body.
It is restless.
It runs away.

You make me stop.
You look at me.
I look at it.
It runs away.

You slow me down.
You make me say.
I will not look.
You will not stop.

I cannot stop.
It helps me do.
I try to speak.
I move too much.

I call you back.
I try to speak.
You can't keep up.
I smile at you.

You look away.
I can't slow down.
I do not know
What I will say.

No Substitute

You are my mother.
You are my friend.
Behold your mother.
Behold your son.

Next week make lamb.
Eat it four days.
Bury the bones.
Eat only berries.

Next week make stew.
Put rabbit in.
Drink the whole thing.
Eat it with bread.

On the third week
Eat only me.
Not me alone.
But eat my love.

You are the lamb.
You are the stew.
Regard your food
before you eat.

Drink only food?
Pour drink on earth.
Then I will live?
Then I will die?

I leave you wood.
I leave you well.
You will require
little more.

On the Folding of the Flag

The room holds the crowd.
Purple and blue open the room.
The body is too large to fit into the body.
No body carries itself.

The flag fills the flag.
All stand.
The folding chairs hold.
His mother is everyone's mother.

Her suit is too straight.
Everyone else is also his mother.
We choose to be here.
The flag fills the cake.

The food is the food people brought.
The sliced fruit is packed-in with cheese cubes.
We keep getting chips.
He brings us all here.

The car doesn't make itself go.
What is it that is stuffed
into the deep fold of the flag
for them to keep forever?

This is

Let there be light.
Let there be forms.
I make the woods.
Let woods make woods.

Let creeks wind through.
Let rocks break ground.
They need no lakes.
They need no pinks.

Three things are all
I need to make.
Each one is good?
Each one makes beings.

Let these see all
as being good.
I shall make them
not see further.

If they seek more
they will not live.
Let them not seek
what we don't make.

You may make pinks.
The wood will fruit.
The light will help
the creeks reveal

what you can see.
What can you see
that you should seek.
And nothing more?

What *you* can make
is something else.

Appliance

We come to talk.
What is TV?
I do not watch
I smile at you.

I work for country.
Receive orders.
I drove one hour
to be here.

How about you?
I like fresh air.
Walked for ten minutes.
Wait for the structure.

How do you feel?
I do not know.
Then make a link.
What do we need?

I am a nurse.
I buy eye shadow.
I buy a ticket.
I am a guest.

Anyone else?
I raise my hand.
I look for hands.
I move my eyes.

You come back up.
Evaluate.
How did it go?
Now it is done.

How do I become
a member?

Smart-Grid

The food *I* eat
comes from the ground
which holds the dead.
and keeps us well.

Look at my dress.
It has a waist.
I walk around.
I wear high heels.

Before today
I could not travel.
Now I have been
to old Peru.

Your time is up.
I have expressed.
I smile at you.
You smile at me.

Now we turn
to speaker 2.
We clear the air
as you walk up.

My family is close-knit.
We watch T.V.
My Dad tests me.
I have been loved.

My lips starlet.
My heart is big.
Those who win here
learn to live long.

The stars live longer
than we do.
They love the world.
We love them back:

And now we turn.
You are a star
though you are wrong.
What about me?

Incarnation

Pretend that this is where we live.
Pretend that we are all the soul.
We have no feet but only moss.
Pretend there are walls.
There are walls.
All we know is all
at once and all we want is what
can hold.

We are within the walls.
The arms and the beds that will hold us dead.
We are the bodies that bring us.
We are the water that feeds us.
The water feeds us bread.
There is no bread that is not the full body.
The body the brain.
The brain the words.
Within.

We are within the water?
We cannot hear what we are within.
Is the body within the brain apart from the body?
Is the brain within the words apart from the brain?
If so the body in the water is apart from the body.
And so the body and so the water the soul.

The Aphids and the Mint

We live on mint.
Let mint make mint.
It is *my* mint.
It is *my* food.

I fill the sink
wash mint of you
so it is cleaned
of those who eat.

We live on mint.
It is not food.
It is too large
for you to clean.

We taste its leaves
as loaves of bread
we could not eat
what is so whole.

This is a mint.
This is its use.
What do you do?
You are not food.

The mint we live.
It is not ours.
It gives: the mint
the mint: we live.

We are: it is.
The leaves the lives
we do not lose.
They are too large.

It is not yours.
We are not ours
but its: Not it
but only its

Not in ourselves.
But with the mint.
We are its.
Now you are not.

Now you are off.
It is all it:
It is for use
and nothing more.

You clean for surface.
The water combs.
The mint remains
a future place.

New Recruits

We gather here for you
Yours are still growing
This is near where we live
Pineapples and strawberries

We are no longer the recruits
We still have files
As do you
What is your question

To anything you might reasonably ask
Ours are unchanging
We are on the website
As are the answers

We keep them that way
The fruits we eat are the ones we choose
We are no longer the recruits
From the fruits that are here

As are the answers
As do you
Why are you thinking of joining
To anything you might reasonably ask

We do not need to want to be here
As do you
Why are you thinking of joining
Pineapples and strawberries

Store (The Poem)

Get the name brand.
Stay with our things.
This is my fruit.
This is the list.

That is your lunch.
We have enough.
Stay with the cart.
Pay while you load.

I want cheerios.
I bring the cart.
No those are bulbs.
Make sure they're there.

This is our cart.
This is my fruit.
We have enough.
Make sure they're there.

This is our cart.
Pay while you load.
I hand you the can.
It is all ours.

Now put on bread.
Don't check the eggs.
Feel for each one.
Make sure they're there.

It is too late.
This one is yours.
If you get lost
Hold on to this.

I Call for Help

I am Amanda.
I cannot do this.
My name is Josh.
I'm here to help.

Type in password.
I do not know.
Make a new one.
Type it again.

Need an update.
Type it again.
It makes me cry.
You are my friend?

I make you laugh.
Type it again.
You help me do.
You understand.

Type it again.
This is our word.
I am your friend.
I am your help.

It does not work.
I come at 8.
I will call you.
When do you sleep?

First thing I'm yours.
While I'm away
Run an update.
Then we can talk.

Part 3

Little Allegory

I run away from
myself there are
foxes and trees
I am
still alive

in my skin warm
I run away from
myself like bark
rubbing
the skin

the skin of the trees
so the foxes are
the ones
that are

now licking below
the hunt and the lady
who runs all stripped

of herself
as I am

of trees.
The foxes
have all
already been
as I in my skin
been here.

Rights

I do not do well without my chattel.
I do not do well without doing what I will with my chattel.
My chattel my bodies my buildings my land.
Do not touch my outermost layer.
It will bite your fingers.
That's how it breathes.

Do not touch my chattel.
It is all fleshy.
All of it counts as one body.
It grows within.
No part breaks off.

Do not extract my chattel.
I do not choose for my parts to be seen.
Because I breed.
Because I breed what I claim

I breed what I do not understand.

Spirit Marker

The only homes are
those I can make
inside of the things that
do not bite

the ears or the hands
having their own
out of which they make
their only homes.

Their homes do not cover
how they live
by the ear
and the hand.

They do not paint
another home
worse by comparison
having only their only homes

they know how that feels.
They trust you to use
your hands to smooth
their walls and their ears.

They are still what they are
in their homes
they can still be made back
into ears into hands.

Scaffold Virus

Build me a house.
My house is small.
It fits *my* kind?
It can't fit yours.

I will not let
us alter plan.
But *I* could make
what fits us both.

You need us both.
I help you make.
My use for you
is only mine

though I prefer
the larger size
I choose the size
I choose the shape.

The kind *I* need?
That is for you.
It fits too much
though space is nice.

I make the house
you tell me to.
I do the work
as though for me.

Your words they help
me make a house.

Heirloom

The girl has nothing but what
she makes: a perfect red dress the story goes.
Then she discovers several.
Indifferently the story says.
The girl who has everything now has nothing but
what she makes.
What she makes is
still the red dress.
She keeps the old
shoes that were
not hers but yours.
The meaningful shoes
that keep her feet over
the earth she never
comes down to
this keeps her poor
it keeps her stuck
in the red dress
while the sky stays
up the sky stays
it never comes down
or forms in clouds
or makes any rain
she drinks only the wine
from the ancestral
store in the goblet
in which it fits.
It does not hold
enough it can never
hold what she is
and yet she can never
add to her store

can never take
what would drain
her of her name
or of the wine
or even of her.

Clothing

You inhabit the body I am too close to inhabit
I am too close to inhabit the violet dress.
You give up your silk and visit the earth
you visit the earth through the distance of knowing
the distance of knowing what you've been and can take off
without the baggage of being the body who auditions

the body who auditions to be the body
even now you shrug in and out and get in deeper
than I who will need like the body to be in
the violet dress again.

Before you discovered your universal
attraction you stood in the row
with the others who were almost
plausible waiting to be asked by the violet dress
by the violet dress it is otherwise wrong to wear
keeping still to keep from tipping over and losing
the violet dress that is stored for the time
of its purpose the violet dress.

I hold myself back
from inhabiting the violet dress
the violet dress laid aside
for the purpose of the violet dress
I inhabit the dress I am too close to inhabit.

My desire does not automatically take
I do not automatically wear the dress.
I give up my old silk through the distance of knowing.

Through Which

Now I am reading
a marriage-plot novel
in order to keep
from being alone.

I say this to you
who refuse
to read Victorian novels
and do not even consider

reading together
the same as being
together
and think that reading differs

from watching
Harry Potter
and seeing the dining
hall triumph

the Hermione anger
and the Ronald charm trip
which neither of us
do not know.

They are like a relationship
for those who are in it
you cannot but know
the communal life

though you refuse
to continue
though you refuse
to spend your whole life

reading marriage-plot novels
or to see what it means
that they are Victorian
and as such can only be

encountered as novels
and as such are better
than *Harry Potter*
for they refuse to stop

being together
and so are more loyal
than a cast of actors
who now get around

and no longer
assemble:
they are like you
in relation to me

off all day doing
experiments
rather than reading
the Victorian novels

through which I make
the community live
through which I keep it
right here.

In Which I Order the Biscuit

I am late getting to The Biscuit
because even though I know where it is
I make myself get lost anyway
by choosing the direction most familiar

along which the sidewalks are coated with ice
the ones I need to traverse to reach
somewhere in Inman which is vaguely where
The Biscuit is which is where I am

meeting the friend I keep waiting
who is a woman increasingly like me
old enough now to get to where I am
tired but satisfied. What else is doing?

Familiar and starting to get what is
satisfied which I know now that I'm here
and my friend gets up to use the restroom
for then I can reach out my boot

until I realize I am making an old woman wait
to get through to her seat
while her daughter orders something to eat.
My outstretched foot welcomes her

sympathetically to complain about having to
wear her boots on the ice
and why oh why do I live here?
which makes me look at her shoes

and admire her laces flat enough
to keep a good pull which makes her affirm
that indeed she is glad to have bought them
and this is where she went to buy them.

And so she goes on until her daughter returns
incidentally putting an end to the words
which I still enjoy now silently talking
while I wait for my friend in the bathroom

others joining the line to complain
about waiting. And when she comes back
we get going. Before we do I ask
which street I should take just to make sure

but mostly to bring in the part
of the city in which I am living.

Apparent Origins

The bust of an elk.
The bust of a brown bear.
The bust of a bighorn sheep.
I know which one is which.
I have seen each kind this year.

The animal skin painted by Native people.
I do not know which ones.
I recognize those are depictions of animals.
I do not know which ones.

Everything else is made of woods that look like trees.
They must be pines.

We are in the mountains.
There are mountains behind the glass.
Those must be the ones.

I am surrounded by all the things here.
I am either in or right near them.
They tell me all I know of them.
They tell me what I need to know.

What the Samsung sees today

The desire today is bread and jam.
They cannot hold it in their hands.
They do not know if it is there.
They feel the possibility.
They have it every other day.
Neither can be had today.

They go out to the store today.
It is the store for bread and jam.
They advertise for it each day.
They touch it with their hands.
There is the possibility
That when they grasp it is not there.

Or if it is, they are not there.
And yet they live to eat today.
They prove the possibility
Of such real things as bread and jam
Of instruments for eating: hands
Or something spread before them: day

They believe in this future day
The future day that is not there
That is not ever in their hands
That they will never call *today*.
That it will end in bread and jam.
That it will end the possibility

That there is no possibility:
That there is no other day
That ever ends in bread and jam.
Never a hope of what's not there
But just another like today
That leaves them sitting with our hands

In front of them with nothing left to do with hands.
We know each possibility.
We know the one they have: today.
We also have all the others' days
To think of as if they were ours
To be unwrapped, their bread, their jam.

Their day and their possibility
One hand there, another there.
Day 1, day 2. *Now* and *then.* Oh bread and jam.

Part 4

Update #1

From many I can make
something.
There is the meeting
in a janitorial gymnasium
with the man who is so great
I am afraid
to miss him.
The dance with my middle-aged grandfather
who is dying
shows me what is off.
There is the art class about
yellow.
The classroom holds its place.
There is a shower door
where water drops confirm the existence
of alien life.
Rabbits in the bush
that won't keep its shape.
There is a wedding in the body
of an actress.
There is an eye doctor's office
where I show up for your appointment.
There is the one where you aren't grateful.
The stupid violent undergraduate play
that makes me angry.
A store that makes me confuse
one and three.
There is a soldier who tells me I should stand
in difficult places.
There is no world that won't be like that
anymore.

Easter Covering

The rabbit in golden foil wrap is valuable in the sense that once it is unwrapped the rabbit will no longer be gold and the foil will no longer be filled. Both will be less than they are now as all of us are without our smooth coverings which we have to get in and in which we cannot remain. So now I have a new dress I wear it three days in a row to keep over the surface of my body and to keep the self within its crisp resplendent fabric that redeems it.

Largesse

I gave twenty-five dollars
for the cupcake
I got for giving
to the ballet.

I wanted to see what
the cupcake
would look like.
I wanted to like it

for being like
being
at the ballet
for even if I could

do ballet
I wouldn't like it
as much I do
when it's the cupcake

on the small plate
with its silver-ball-
sprinkled-and-lavender
frosting

that keeps it
from being just food
that keeps it
as long I eat it

floating like light in the liking mind.

Self-Having

My bra is fresh washed
and smells of fresh scent
as my hair smells
of the cucumber-mint

conditioner
custom ordered
as a gift
for my type of hair

and so I may as well
use it and smell
of what has been given
and feel

that everything
that smells is given
like their scents
and so my skin and so my hair

feel as though
they were given
and so the world
out the window

that is even less given
for it smells
of itself
as we all must do

though this does not happen
whenever we can
be washed
or dressed or inside

and so given
by scents
to ourselves
and our sense of their having

Removing Degrees

The man I live
with looks like his
brother
who back in the day

would have stepped in
if an emergency
should happen. But
today my brother-in-law

sits far away
on the couch in
no place to say
anything of our life

he looks like a boy
in my class who
looks up and is
listening but may

or may not approve.
He likes to raise
objections and have them
righted. It's really

just that my brother-in-law
and the boy
in my class look
alike to a degree

that supposing there
could only be
two brothers
would shut out my

lover and me.
They are two brothers
with whom
we have nothing to do.

Metaphysical Complaint on Ash Wednesday

When Valentine's Day and Ash Wednesday overlap with the black lace pinned over the red the black does not subsume the red but makes it sexy like date night. If red is tacked over black then Christ on the cross becomes a Valentine's card that is country-brand corny and thus a less sexy version of date night, a date without my godless husband who especially hates country songs about Jesus. His aversion usually prevents me from desecrating my religion as St Valentine's Feast threatens to do. Keep it from meaning. Keep from wearing a black date night dress or red to go with ashes. Keep from doing what I wish since I love all layers of meaning. I especially love the meanings of colors and every effusion in which they get lost.

●

Ashes. When I nod down the path I disgruntle a man, occasioning words: "At first there was bestiality, and then the women started walking around on God's earth." And I like the feeling of being off the spectrum of man and his animals: who knows what I will do with the words one might say as one walks decently along speaking the truths that keep their own council not bothering any who doesn't butt in? What business *do* I have being friendly? Smiling at my fellow creatures, looking just as I would if I looked at myself in the mirror.

●

A romantic effusion. This is not about me he says. This is about me and you. Like anyone else I would be nice if you weren't that way that doesn't let me be who I am for who I am in my heart would never do anything bad by you.

I would not do what you make me do. I would never do anything less than you deserve and you would have no grounds for complaint if the world were such as the world should be and such as it needs for the proper function of you. If the world were that way there would be no obliging those who would have you otherwise than at heart you really are.

For in your heart through which I know who you are *I* am your life. That is why being together is getting down to the basics of you. Getting down into where we are bodies together and when you get up I can never be right.

Shower Hat

I take the box and hand it
to Margaret
while the friend
tapes the bows

on the paper plate.
Some of them turn out
like curls
until it is like

the whole living room
covered
with centerpiece
flowers and marriage initials

in wedding colors
all over the rented tables
and counters.
Then at the end

of the day
we all sit around
to say how special
the day

and the centerpieces
and how hard the week
for there was a student of Margaret's
who pushed her

for Margaret made her
sing after her father
cut off her curls
for their tradition

and Margaret didn't know
what to say
and so she decided
to compliment

her new hair
so the little girl
pushed her and bruised her
fair skin

so now Margaret lifts
her freshly colored hair
to show us the mark
the girl made

in wonder that
a girl that age
should have done such a thing
to her teacher.

She wonders at
the cutting of the hair
and we wonder along
and get a new plate

as is our ritual.

Picking Up Pete

I learn today about pets
from the sweetness of men
one of whom I briefly see.
Another is Pete

the boyfriend of
my friend. She asked me
to go with him
to his surgery I think

because I have my own
person and care for him
though I have never
done that with him.

I discover when I sit
next to Pete
as "a steadying presence"
the feeling of care is

completely transitive.
It only becomes
different when it leads to
his features that differ:

the joke about not
being nervous
and the physical fact
of glasses and the lank

blond hair
that makes him different
from my husband
and therefore from me.

Makes a point of leaving
his bag with me
picking it up
and then coming back

to put it back down
another acknowledgment
of need of care.
Or am I making

too much of this
aspect of surgery
of not taking anything
or anyone

with you. Even if someone
is there for you,
more than willing.
Why do I latch on

to caring
for those when they
do not especially need
me to care

and would not
let me really?
Would not even let me
touch them.

Tentative like other people-
's pets. They
understand.
I reach for them

then stop half way.

Walking Love Object

A very common name
can be dehumanizing
it is like walking into the room
with a shoe affixed to your paw

or a bow to your ear
which says I'm a girl
that is how it feels
to be named Amanda

a word which means
worthy of love
which made me dread
the Latin class

in which the professor was sure
to point it out:
the one in which
we would cover "deserving to be loved."

My name automatically
raises the question
do you agree? as for some reason
when I turned twenty-one

my friend had me
walk around making people
kiss me and I still walk around
saying my name

as a question
or maybe it's an apology
for answering to such a thing
which used to mean

I am a man
but now it means
I make you feel—
that is what I think I am.

Favor Envelope

I want to make this
easy for you
for I know you are trying
to ask for a favor:

a certain letter
is needed for law school.
Let us sit under
the redbud tree.

I give you something
different to say.
What are you writing
your thesis about?

It always takes longer
than one would like.
 "I am writing about
Virginia Woolf and in particular

Mrs. Dalloway and the fact that it lasts
only one day
and why the length of
a day is important."

Why does it always take longer
than I would like?
To show that I am
a granter of favors

I help you with the paper
I show you the envelope,
but still we sit under
the redbud again?

What is the frame
around the day?
What determines
when it is over?

Why does it always take longer
than you would like?
Now as an opening
for the letter

I ask you
What are you doing next summer?
Is this taking longer
than you would like?

"I am actually
applying for law school
and I actually need
your letter."

Of course I will
and I look forward
to writing for someone
I know so well.

But it always takes longer
than I would like.
You start to rise
but I keep you at bay

I actually lean back
and take a loud breath
to express my admiration
for the redbud tree

to keep you sitting
until we have reached
the time for standing.
For I now learn

it is not just
up to me
to decide
to make this easy

in my new-revealed nature
as a granter of favors
it is apparently
my vocation

to serve as
an enveloper
and to connect others
so I will have to

have you over
for dinner
for my husband
would so love

to meet you
though your role in my life
is now over
though the day is early

and is not yet over
and we cannot stand
until we have finished
our dinner

even in order
to write the letter
for that is how
 an envelope works.

It never takes longer
than a full day.
But it always takes longer
than you would like.

Taken Up Short or

Leaning over the pew in front
impatient for it to end *come on*
do you really expect me to?
I remind myself of the portrait

at the Denver Impressionists exhibit
of a woman who is dying which I knew
before I read the inscription
by the way she averts her face

from whoever is looking
which means she is above caring
who it is or how
which brings me back to

this church where I bring
my body, enabling it to be seen
which makes me have to convey with my face
I am here in spite of that.

Now a man shiftlessly looks back toward me
my expression averts and
I'm holy—there is no
one who will meet my eye.

I also cannot look at any of them.
If I did I would lose this
I do not know what will happen to me
though you do. I can't.

If we looked at each other
I would be more like the woman I saw
in a documentary about her likely death
who during the brief

span when she thought
she was out of the woods posed
for the advertisement playfully
covered with only an x-ray image of her chest

as I later found out
she was wrong.
What difference does it make?
What difference does it make now?

Twenty-Eight

At twenty-eight
my mother got pregnant
which means that she
would go on to be

mother of "the twins"
successful in school
I am not sure
how that affected her.

At fifty-six now
she still has twins
she still has one
that is in school.

I am still calling
her to complain
about school
and not doing as well.

But today is different for me
for today I am twenty-eight.
I do not call
but think of my mother

back at the time
when she was my age
the age she was when I was born
back when she was

married six years
was an accountant
and felt like herself
trim in her cute

red and black suit
smart enough
she especially liked
the part of the job where

she went out to lunch
which she still does
without the job
and still enjoys it

now that we are gone
and in that sense grown up.
And now that I'm grown
to the age that she was

just before we existed
when she felt like herself
I look in the mirror
put on a skirt-suit

she might have worn
go out to lunch
where I feel
like myself

and suddenly I am
neither of us
I am neither
one of the twins

nor their mother
but her
before she was
a mother

or maybe me
before I was
whatever it is
that I have been.

First Words

It is not the case that this language is doing anything in particular. This is it. It is the language I use to understand literature and also the language from the loud-speaker in the car that keeps driving by repeating itself. It is the language we use to think about how what comes in and out of consciousness when we would rather not be awake feels true in a way that's a violation of what should be the case if what we are trying to understand were made for that.

Bakers

Now today. Today you will bake
a new kind of bread. The one with
the layers and the uncertain
number of rolls and the certain

kind of hazelnut filling.
It will be enough like the bread
that you know for it to have dough
into which you can knead

the part of the task that you need
to work out. For however new
there is nothing so hard it cannot
get absorbed and once it gets in

it will bake right back out.
We will make sure there is nothing
so new it is not old enough
for there to be parts you already

know to which you can return
as you will to your home at the end
of the day to say I am here
to the ones who are there.

At very worst you will have to say,
"That was a day. I did not do
what I should have been able."

It Will Work Out

My sister decided it would work out
when she decided to have a baby
and to marry the man who fathered the baby
if they made it happen then it would work out

as happened today when my aunt Maggie
had surgery to extract her ovaries
when the doctor said it could be cancer
she worried then figured it would work out

and then it did though it took more out
of her than she had expected.
What range is there of things
working out? When my sister says

it will work out she means
a life that does not come apart
and a lack of postpartum feeling
but I do not think she admits what she means.

How do the words make the mind stay put? I ask
as I put off the non-invasive procedure
for clearing myself of uterine lining
I do not believe would do any good.

I do not even think it would help me
give birth though my sister will
and Aunt Maggie had three that came out
after growing in her like cysts.

What would it mean to say they turned out?
Will what has been keep working out?
I wonder if my sister's confidence in life
comes from the belief she could have come out

of anything. In thinking that my sister believes
there is a general ability to give birth
an ability to make lives that work out
like surgeries.

Talking Reason

There is a man with whom I share a music pamphlet at church who is dressed in a way that makes me wonder if he is poor and then twenty minutes afterwards I see him reading Plato in front of a store but I am not completely sure it is the same person. I am also still not sure whether he is homeless so I come up and ask if he is the person I was with at church and he looks up at me very kindly and says yes. I want to ask him how he is doing but I never do because instead I ask if he is a student and he says yes at MIT and I think he knows that I have come up to him for a reason which he deflects by asking me if I am a student which means he is also getting his bearings and he looks at the bottom of my flower-spangled dress poking out from under my coat. I am afraid he thinks my being nicely dressed has something to do with my reason for coming up to him. But in what sense? He does not tell me but asks what I study so I ask him what he does and when he says physics I mention that my husband also studies that but bringing him up as I have been doing these days for some reason makes me fear this man thinks I came up to him for a different reason.

Intervention

I want to intervene
by asking a poet I know
if he is doing okay
but when I am honest

I know that writing about
wanting to die
does not mean
you actually want that

or that you think
about what it would actually mean
but I still
want to intervene

because I want him
not to want to die
even in the way you can
make yourself feel that

in writing about it
which gives me this desire
to intervene taking
the question of what

he feels in writing about it
as an opening
to think about what it means
when it is not happening

only in writing
but to make the feeling
a vulnerable thing
said to someone

taking that seriously.
I would intervene
if I could do such a thing
not to ignore

the fact of his writing
but to force
an encounter with the person
who does that.

Name-Thing

Trying to pass whatever
flowers there are I walk by
witch-hazel
without being sure

what witch-hazel is
or without being sure
what this shrub is called
depending on which

is taken to be more
important but
anyway witch-hazel
is the name of a yellow

flowering shrub
that grows in Cambridge
in early spring
which I know for sure

whether or not
this is one because
unless something is
a tulip or a daffodil

I cannot be sure
but the possibility is
enough to be
a thing the name is for

a possibility which is
something to put out there
like a plant
that is worth walking by

because it signifies that
now it is spring.

Part 5

Loved Self

day seems gorgeous to me beyond what it is which I can tell because being out here makes me think of my own body and I feel gorgeous in the cold air just for having legs and hair in which to catch the sun and cold. I realize this again when I come in and see my caramel-colored sandals and perceiving them is looking down at my own feet which they make gorgeous or the other way around I cannot tell which is how it works so I will never know the value that anything has without me in it which could make me sad but how else so I may as well be in love with myself in a way that is not like looking in the mirror but instrumental like being married or believing in God. In love with myself through which the world acquires its quality and the day and the body through which the self acquires its.

Limit Objects

The paint on my pencil is how to spark the gold like lichen green on the rocks around here and the other speckles are burnt as in orange duck legs so they can come in too. And hair slightly twisted in the ponytail holder is how to get the shape of the fallen trunk of tree but what color is it like? How does it connect to self-extent? The graphite tip of this pencil. That's how. But why does it work like that? Why am I not allowed to see past what other objects are already doing which can never be everything and sometimes even when they can be seen do not register.

•

Except for self-extent I have not registered. A pumpkin is how. It stands in the field with its orifices cut out, enabling flame. It has been placed inside a face. Like me. Thus the pumpkin affords the time and the pie around which I can then gather those like me who do not think far into the future for we prefer to eat pumpkin pie and live in these pieces of pie—is it stale?—for as long as it pleases. Having a face is like eating an apple to which I am allergic. But eating pie is like looking at faces.

•

Faces bring in the body and the special course in which we learn how to inhabit it. I am instructed that I am a jellyfish and the air is ocean and then I love having a body for it is fun to fill with wave that flows the way I open-swim with anus-mouth. Slowly undulating my arms as if it is harder to move them. Being a diaphanous fish is how I get to what I want in the bag of candy. That is the point of it. But I do not get into it because my body lacks the weight and flavor of candy which makes me as wistful as I have ever felt about anything else, as I fill the pages to get myself feeling like breathing in order to move.

●

Feeling makes the movement that brings objects with it. This feeling makes me get up to move my purse as if it could suddenly be in the way where I sit. This means that where I am enables me to walk to the park outside where there are people. Which puts within reach the gingerbread people. Each is a person I know: the man and the woman. And so the woman I love in addition to my husband is differently real in scent of emotion from my male husband who loves the winter and is real like *really*, like *why does it matter?* Then winter can give way to the warmth of moving nearer to what is uneven in all of them which is also an object.

Limit Objects 2

Iridescent like objects. The pine needles glimmer with white sunlight as if they have caught wool from the backs of the oxen in the myth. The oxen enable me to make out the blond ponies that trail everything behind them. Though I only see one now I know from its assurance they come in clusters that can be seen as quick as their glitter that keeps you from seeing what else they are. What else they are invites what else there is that looks like it's alive.

●

I participate just enough. I keep myself dry where I keep myself above the waves where they lap. The aqua keeps below the black above the water that's the color of water. Between them the incarnation of self as an object. What else? The self as an object that is used for its iridescence like these words that make you feel you have to do something to yourself with them. They are said when I am a bridesmaid and comprise the speech for which I get an unlit candle. I am not told what to do with the candle or with its white concrete border printed with mauve roses and with the words *New York Botanical Garden.*

●

Objects are not iridescent. They are self-contained and I don't have to do anything with them. More like the color of the faded chapter I have been writing than the color of the Rothko painting I tried to walk into like the description said. The difficult red gives way to the hut by Monet that looks like it is made of lilac mud where all I have to do is absorb what everyone loves. This accessibility enables me to make out smaller objects easily. Turns on the high-definition documentary in which ice crackles to freeze cabbage leaves that huddle to center then settle down like metaphors.

•

The metaphors into which objects have settled after acquiring artificial luminescence demand an act of analysis. I hold them in my mind to put back into them what they make me feel—save it for later. The act of preservation conjures the apple I save for later which I eat each day with peanut butter even though I am allergic to apples. This choice of snack enables me to hear my mother ignore the diagnosis. Does such behavior on the part of a mother regarding an apple warrant an act of analysis? The iridescence of objects primarily suited for eating has yet to be proven.

Limit Objects 3

Christmas Day. The lavender and tea tree oil soap I get enables me to remember the fleecy pajama bottoms I also get. Then all the other clothes line up to give themselves to me by being equally new to wear. They promise me that I will be. In enough of them I can walk outside which enables me to escape from the sound of the snowmelt on the roof of the apartment and the stupid suspense of not knowing where it will currently happen. Once I am outside I can then pick a place to which I can go and order chai tea.

●

Walking enables me to get to the plane in which I can fly to the destination of the vacation I have ordered. The vacation includes the view from the plane window of the pink strip of sunset over the river. I look over the shoulder of the casual blond woman in the window seat who vexes until my visible pleasure causes her to take in the view for herself and tap a picture. The features of the plane are what we pay for without thinking. They enable us to get something out of it that is not what we pay for. Arriving at my destination makes me want to go camping closer to home. I do bringing food from the store to avoid places where objects are ordered.

●

I devote myself to the objects that lack features no one would pay for. Hence my love of books that are said to be meaningful. One of these is *Wuthering Heights* in which I anticipate the lone bluebell standing in the appropriate landscape before I get to the part where Catherine and Nelly see that very bluebell. The bloom brings with it the patch from which it naturally arises which "clouded the turf steps with a lilac mist." This imaginary profusion of nature that cannot be paid for then summons the river of lavender ice in which I see my own perceiving. What is underneath I cannot tell. Whatever it is looks red and green.

●

The objects that lack features I would not pay for begin to make me superstitious as if they suppress them. An example is the lightbulbs that go off in order to work again like that has not happened. What is mysterious enables replacement. This brings forth the gold-yellow blooms of the begonia and the leaves of the mint that replace themselves. They touch each other. We get what we pay for which raises the question of what else we are getting. Do the hidden parts of objects know each other? I choose to believe they do. Then their knowledge of each other enables those I wish to have over to come in with them.

Limit Objects 4

I am confused by the objects I am led through: meadow, meadow, and gate. They give way to the woods that further scare and solidify me through their trees which are copies that displace former copies. The twitching of the light through the trees enables me to become the rabbit I need to be in order to survive the repetition. Becoming a particular animal leads the trees to become distinct. They differ as much as eyes differ from apples. The comparison between eyes and apples displaces me. This comparison which is not my own is more than possible.

●

I help make others' words and also dinner. I cannot do I only help. I cut the stems. I soap and rinse. The reason I can only help is that I am made for this alone. My overarching sense of purpose enables the death of Christ, fills in the gap in the practice conversation, and refills the pineapples and strawberries that help recruit more members to the groups we are in. All have reference to the afterlife. My concern regarding this enables me to reach out to those who reassure in the words they have to hold.

●

In speaking I breed what I do not understand because the words are not here for their own meaning. They are those that can be made into the homes I know how to make. The homes are what we need to smooth our walls and our ears. They come with the arms and the beds that will hold us dead and the water that feeds us bread. The arms also come with the Samsung that stores our days and offers us our bread our jam. It speaks the words that needs have brought into my existence.

•

As the owner of a home filled with objects I acquire largesse. I attend weddings, donate, and savor experiences that float like light in the liking mind. I even savor surgeries because they have worked out and afford opportunities for caring which I also enjoy. Another opportunity occurs in the form of intervening words that do not need to be spoken. Such words enable possibilities which signify the existence of their conditions. Possibilities summon the tulips, The Biscuit, all non-chocolate rabbits, and the apartment that now exist in Cambridge.

•

What now exists is not just Cambridge and the objects that are in it. The gorgeous day and the body with hair and legs also exist more generally. They bring the atmosphere. To say that objects are general feels true in a way that violates what should be the case. Violating what should be the case I step into the crispness of the gingham dress. It is white and black checked in a way that connects what are localized beyond redemption.

Acknowledgments

"A Story," *Harvard Review Online*

"Green Proofs," *The Colorado Review*

"The Eve Virus," *Conjunctions* (online)

"Hospice Bot," *Conjunctions* (online)

"Conveyor," *Conjunctions* (online)

"Apollo to Daphne," *Conjunctions* (online)

"On the Folding of the Flag," *Poetry Northwest*

"This is," *Conjunctions* (online)

"Appliance," *Boston Review*

"Smart-Grid," *Boston Review*

"Incarnation," *Conjunctions* (online)

"The Aphids and the Mint," *Fence*

"New Recruits," *Boston Review*

"Little Allegory," *Denver Quarterly*

"Rights," *Paris Review*

"Heirloom," *Conjunctions* (online)

"Update #1," *The Colorado Review*

"Largesse," *The Colorado Review*

"Self-Having," *Kenyon Review*

"Removing Degrees," *Kenyon Review*

Excerpts from "The Great Ones," *Thrush Poetry Journal*

Excerpts from "Kept Dry," *Denver Quarterly*

C&R PRESS TITLES

NONFICTION

Women in the Literary Landscape by Doris Weatherford, et al
Credo: An Anthology of Manifestos & Sourcebook for Creative Writing by Rita Banerjee and Diana Norma Szokolyai

FICTION

Last Tower to Heaven by Jacob Paul
No Good, Very Bad Asian by Lelund Cheuk
Surrendering Appomattox by Jacob M. Appel
Made by Mary by Laura Catherine Brown
Ivy vs. Dogg by Brian Leung
While You Were Gone by Sybil Baker
Cloud Diary by Steve Mitchell
Spectrum by Martin Ott
That Man in Our Lives by Xu Xi

SHORT FICTION

Notes From the Mother Tongue by An Tran
The Protester Has Been Released by Janet Sarbanes

ESSAY AND CREATIVE NONFICTION

the internet is for real by Chris Campanioni
Immigration Essays by Sybil Baker
Je suis l'autre: Essays and Interrogations
by Kristina Marie Darling
Death of Art by Chris Campanioni

POETRY

A Family Is a House by Dustin Pearson
The Miracles by Amy Lemmon
Banjo's Inside Coyote by Kelli Allen
Objects in Motion by Jonathan Katz
My Stunt Double by Travis Denton
Lessons in Camoflauge by Martin Ott
Millennial Roost by Dustin Pearson
Dark Horse by Kristina Marie Darling
All My Heroes are Broke by Ariel Francisco
Holdfast by Christian Anton Gerard
Ex Domestica by E.G. Cunningham
Like Lesser Gods by Bruce McEver
Notes from the Negro Side of the Moon by Earl Braggs
Imagine Not Drowning by Kelli Allen
Notes to the Beloved by Michelle Bitting
Free Boat: Collected Lies and Love Poems by John Reed
Les Fauves by Barbara Crooker
Tall as You are Tall Between Them by Annie Christain
The Couple Who Fell to Earth by Michelle Bitting
Notes to the Beloved by Michelle Bitting